FUN WITH ASTRONOMY

ASTRONOMY

by *MAE* and *IRA FREEMAN*

RANDOM HOUSE · NEW YORK

ACKNOWLEDGMENTS

Except where otherwise noted, the photographs are by the authors. The boy in the pictures is their son, John Blacker Freeman, nine years old.

The authors wish to express their thanks for the use of astronomical photographs to: Mount Wilson and Palomar Observatories, pages 6, 31-C, 31-D, 33-D, 51-B, 52, 57-B; Official U. S. Navy Photograph, Navy Department, pages 8, 11-A; Yerkes Observatory, pages 18, 21, 33-A, 33-B, 33-C, 40, 43-A, 43-B, 61-E; American Museum of Natural History, pages 23-A, 39; High Altitude Observatory of Harvard University and the University of Colorado, page 43-C; Lowell Observatory, pages 31-A, 31-B.

CONTENTS

This telescope at Mount Palomar Observatory in California is the biggest in the world. At the bottom of the big steel framework is the mirror used to gather light from the stars. It is 17 feet across. The mirror alone weighs 14½ tons, and its mounting weighs 500 tons, yet the whole telescope can be moved by a motor as small as the one on an electric fan.

INTRODUCTION

If you look at the sky on a clear night you will be able to understand why astronomy has interested people ever since ancient times. The beauty of the brilliant stars, the gleaming planets and the silvery moon brings us a feeling of wonder and makes us want to find out as much as we can about everything in the sky. And what has been found out is not only interesting itself, but is very important and helpful to other sciences like navigation and weather study.

An astronomer no longer spends most of his time looking through a telescope. Instead, he usually attaches a camera to it to get a permanent picture that can be studied. Sometimes astronomers hook other instruments to the telescope to examine the light of the stars and planets in order to find out what they are made of and how fast they are moving.

Astronomy makes a good hobby and there are amateur astronomy clubs all over the world where children as well as grown-ups work on interesting projects. In the United States, nearly 50,000 people have built their own telescopes. They report what they see to the big observatories and in this way are very helpful to professional astronomers.

Have you ever visited a planetarium? Do so if you can, because there you can watch the movements of artificial stars, sun, moon and planets as they shine on a dome-like movie screen overhead.

This book will help you find out some interesting things about what there is in the sky, so turn the page and begin to have some "Fun with Astronomy."

Just a few years ago, astronomers found that some stars send out radio waves as well as light. This huge instrument, located on top of the Naval Research Laboratory near Washington, is called a radio telescope. The hollow reflector is 50 feet across and catches radio waves just as the mirror of the Mount Palomar telescope gathers light waves.

ABOUT THE EARTH

A long time ago people thought that the earth was the center of everything. The stars, planets, sun and moon all seemed to circle around the firm, solid earth on which they lived. If you asked what held the earth up, they would tell you that it rested on the back of a huge elephant. If you wanted to know what held the elephant up, they would say that he stood on the shell of a giant turtle. And that is about as far as their "explanation" went.

Nowadays we know that the earth is not held up by anything, that it is round and moves through space in a special way. It is one of nine planets that move around the sun, and our sun is only one of thousands of billions of billions of others that we know about. Since we live on the earth and can move around on it, we can find out a great deal about astronomy and especially about the other planets by studying the earth first.

People have known for more than 2,000 years that the earth is round rather than flat. They found this out by noticing that when a ship sails out to sea the hull disappears from view first, then the sails, and finally the top of the mast is completely hidden behind the round bulge of the earth. What seems to be the farthest rim of the earth as you look out over the ocean or over flat land is called the *horizon*.

By measuring how much the earth's surface curves, scientists have found that it is a ball about 7,900 miles through the middle. Three-quarters of it is covered by the sea. Valleys and mountains on the land are only small wrinkles compared with the large size of the ball. And around the whole earth is a thin film of air.

For a very long time after it became known that the world is round, people still believed that it was the center of everything in the sky. This was natural because on a clear night the stars really do seem to be lights that are fastened into a rounded dome, and this dome appears to turn slowly from east to west as the night passes. The true reason for this is the spinning of the earth itself, just as when you ride on a merry-go-round it seems as though the things on the ground are all turning in the opposite direction.

Billions of years ago, the earth was started spinning in this way and has kept on ever since, just because there is nothing out in space to stop it. The imaginary rod around which the globe turns is called its *axis*. One end of the axis is called the North Pole and the other is the South Pole.

If you have never noticed how the whole sky seems to move, you can check it in just a few minutes on any clear evening. Face toward the south and choose your position so that the corner of a house is on your right. Keep your head from moving by lying on the ground or sitting back in a chair as John is doing in the picture. Pick a star that is very close to the edge of the wall and watch it steadily. After a minute or two you will see it disappear behind the house.

While making daily turns, the earth also makes a trip around the sun once a year. It moves along a huge, slightly flattened circle 186,-000,000 miles wide at a speed of more than 18 miles a second. So just while you have been reading this paragraph we have all moved along through space about 500 miles. The other planets also move around the sun but on different paths, taking different times to do so.

These overlapping pictures were taken from a V-2 rocket 100 miles up. The curve of the horizon shows that the earth is really round. The white woolly spots are clouds, and the dark strip at the left is the Gulf of Mexico.

Keep your head steady to see the stars move.

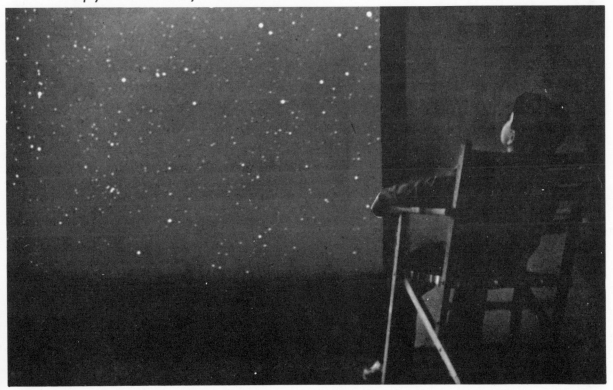

THE SEASONS

The movement of the earth around the sun causes the changing seasons. You will see how this happens by doing an experiment in a darkened room.

For the earth, use a plain-colored rubber ball, and stick a knitting needle through the middle to be the axis on which the earth spins. Mark the *equator*, which is the imaginary line around the middle of the globe. Stick a lump of modeling clay into a small board and push the needle into the clay to hold the ball on a slant, as in the picture. Use a bare lamp as the sun, and place the "earth" off to one side with the needle tilted toward the lamp. This is where the earth is on June 21st every year.

Turn on the lamp and you will see that just half the earth is lighted by the sun. As the earth turns, all places above the equator spend more time on the light side than on the dark side. This is why, in summer, the days are longer than the nights. In the southern half of the world things are just the opposite. In June, Australia is having its winter.

Next, see what happens half a year later, about December 21st, by moving the ball to the opposite side of the lamp. The needle should now be tipped directly *away* from the lamp, because when the earth goes around the sun its axis always keeps the same direction in space. Now the northern half of the world is having winter, with shorter days and longer nights, while the southern half of the world is having summer.

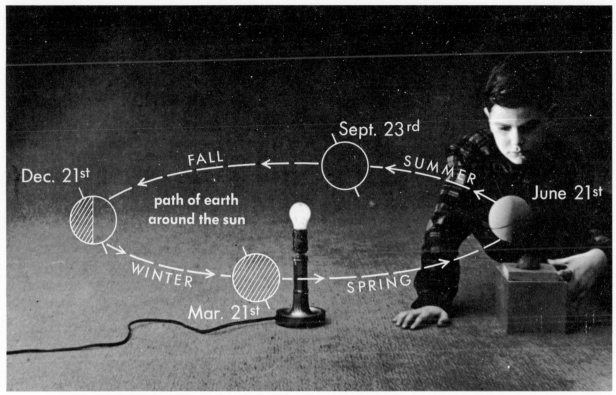

The slant of the earth's axis makes the seasons change.

Dec. 21st

FALL

Sept. 23rd

SUMMER

June 21st

path of earth
around the sun

WINTER

Mar. 21st

SPRING

The earth on June 21st.

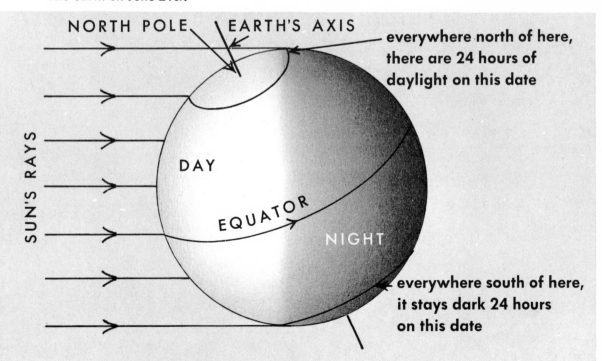

NORTH POLE

EARTH'S AXIS

everywhere north of here,
there are 24 hours of
daylight on this date

SUN'S RAYS

DAY

EQUATOR

NIGHT

everywhere south of here,
it stays dark 24 hours
on this date

The picture also shows where the earth is on September 23rd and on March 21st. On these two dates all parts of the world have exactly twelve hours of daylight and twelve hours of darkness. Check this by putting the ball in each of these places.

The experiment with the ball showed that because the earth's axis slants, we have longer days in summer than in winter. This is one reason why we get much more heat from the sun in summer. But the slant of the axis does something else that makes summer days hotter. You can find this out by another experiment.

Cut out the top and bottom of a tin can and give one side of each piece a coat of stove polish or other *dull* black paint. After the paint has dried, set the pieces out in the sun with one facing directly toward the sun while the other is placed so that the sunlight hits it on a slant, as in the picture. After about ten minutes, touch the two lids, one after the other, to your arm and you will notice that the one that faced squarely into the sun feels much hotter than the other.

This is exactly what happens to any piece of ground on the earth. The drawing on the opposite page shows that in summer the sun's rays hit the ground more squarely than they do in winter, and this is the main reason for the difference between summer and winter weather. Through the whole year, the equator gets about $2\frac{1}{2}$ times as much heat from the sun as the North Pole does.

If the axis of the earth happened to be straight up instead of slanting, there would be no changing seasons, and each place on earth would have about the same kind of weather all the year round.

The lid on the left gets much hotter.

A slanting beam of sunlight spreads thinner than a direct one.

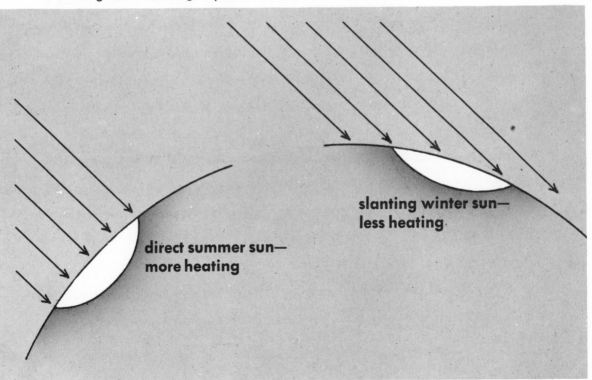

direct summer sun—
more heating

slanting winter sun—
less heating

TELLING TIME

The sun, as it crosses the sky each day, gives us a way of keeping time. Long ago, people decided to divide each day into 24 equal parts, called hours, and to break up each hour into 60 minutes and each minute into 60 seconds.

Because the sun moves across the sky toward the west, noontime will come later for people living west of you and earlier for those east of you. Our country is so large that it is divided into four parts, each with its own time, as the map on the opposite page shows.

Our watches and clocks are just handy machines that are made to keep step with the sun. Before these were invented, people often used sundials to tell time.

Make your own sundial. Get a piece of board about 10 inches square and paint it white. Make a saw-cut ¼ inch deep across the middle of the board, keeping the saw straight up and down. From a piece of thin plywood, cut a triangle of the shape shown in the drawing. Fit the triangle into the groove on the board. Now set the sundial on a post outdoors where it will be in the sun. The lower point of the triangle must face south. Be sure that the board is level but do not fasten it down yet.

Exactly at noon on a sunny day, turn the board until the shadow of the triangle becomes a thin line that falls straight back along the groove. You can now nail the board in place. Remember that if your town is on Daylight Saving Time you must set the board this way when your watch says one o'clock.

At each hour during the day draw a line to mark the shadow position and put the hour number on each line according to sun time.

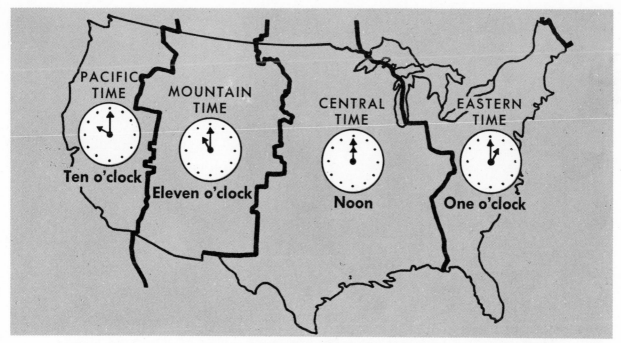

This is the way our country is divided in order to keep closer to sun time. When it is four o'clock in New York it is only one o'clock in California.

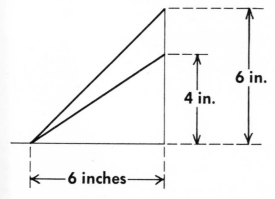

If you live in the northern half of the United States, make the triangle 6 inches high. If you live in the southern half, make it 4 inches high.

The finished sundial.

This picture, taken through a large telescope, shows how the moon would look if it were only 3,000 miles away.

THE MOON

The starting signal is given. Outside there is a blinding glare of orange-colored light and a thunderous, roaring blast. You feel the back of your seat pushing on you like a giant's hand. You have just taken off on a rocket trip to the moon! Of course, right now this is something we can do only in imagination.

Long before there was any serious talk of rocket ships, astronomers had found out a great many things about the moon. We know that it is a ball about one-fourth as wide as the earth. Even though it is our nearest neighbor in the sky, it is almost a quarter of a million miles away. The moon goes around the earth on an oval path, just as the earth moves around the sun on a much larger oval path. Other planets besides the earth have moons too. One of them has as many as twelve.

Suppose your rocket ship has just made a safe landing on the moon. You and the other passengers cannot simply step out of the door and walk away from the ship, for conditions on the moon are very different from those on earth. First of all, there is no air on the moon so you would have to furnish your own supply from a tank of compressed air strapped to your back. You would be wearing a special "space suit" to keep your body at the air pressure you are used to on earth. You would also have to carry an electric battery to furnish power for air-conditioning your suit because wherever the sun is shining directly the temperature will be much higher than boiling water, but in the shade it will go down to around 180 degrees below zero.

The reason we do not have such extreme temperatures on earth is that our air and water spread out the sun's heat. Because the moon has no air or water, there are no clouds, no winds, no storms and no sounds. And the sun and stars shine out in a perfectly black sky all the time because there is no air to scatter their direct rays and so light up the sky, as on earth.

In exploring this strange world, you would have to climb over rough, jagged rocks, and all around would be high, steep mountains and ridges. The ground would be crisscrossed with huge, deep cracks and underfoot everywhere there would be several inches of white dust, like flour.

Right from the beginning of your moon hike, you would certainly notice how easy it is to walk along even over the rough trail. With every step you would find yourself sailing several feet into the air in a sort of slow-motion broad jump. This is because the moon is so much smaller than the earth that the pull of its gravity is only about one-sixth as strong. If you were to step onto a scale while on the moon, you would find your weight to be scarcely twelve pounds there! By this time you would probably be willing to climb back into your space ship and return to earth where things seem more normal.

The moon is too small and far away to have much effect on our earth except for its gravity pull on the ocean. This causes the tides, making the water level rise a few feet as the moon comes overhead. But there is no scientific proof of any effect of the moon on people, plants or animals.

Craters and mountains on the moon. The big crater is 64 miles across.

A CLOSE-UP OF THE CRATERS

If you could really go to the moon you would find that most of the larger mountains are the rims of great hollow craters, sometimes with sharp peaks sticking up from the center. The picture on page 12, taken through a large telescope, shows how rough most of the moon's surface is. The darker parts are smooth, rock-like material that looks dark because it does not reflect as much light as the powdery dust around it.

Astronomers cannot say exactly what caused the craters. Some think they were made by explosions from inside the moon, like the volcanoes on earth. Others believe they were made by large meteors that crashed into the moon ages ago, and you can see how this might happen by trying an experiment.

Dig up a couple of handfuls of earth that has no stones in it. Mix with water in a tin can, adding the water a little at a time, stirring all the while, until you have a "gooey" mud. It should be fairly thick so that when some is pushed aside it does not flow back. Pour most of the mud onto a large flat plate. Shake the plate with a round-and-round motion to make the mud spread all over it in an even, thin layer. Now drop bits of the remaining mud from a knife held about two feet above the plate. You will see that the splash holes look very much like the craters on the moon. Some even have a peak in the middle!

Astronomers have counted about 30,000 craters on the moon, from small ones only about 100 feet wide to giant ones much more than 100 miles across, some with rims 2 miles high. The larger craters can be seen with an ordinary field glass.

Meteor Crater in Arizona, as seen from an airplane. It is almost a mile wide.

Drop bits of mud from the knife . . .   . . . to get these "splash craters."

FINDING THE DISTANCE

Because astronomers cannot actually stretch a tape measure from here to the moon, they must find this distance in some roundabout manner. Surveyors use a special way to measure distances on earth, and astronomers use the same idea to figure out how far away things are in the sky.

One astronomer goes to an observatory north of the equator, say at Boston, while his partner goes to one that is south of the equator such as the one at Capetown in South Africa, over 6,000 miles away. At an exact moment arranged in advance, they sight on the moon. Each one notes the place where the moon seems to be against the faraway stars. From the difference in these two positions, the distance to the moon can be figured out. The distance to the sun or to some of the nearer stars can be found in a similar way.

Perhaps you would like to try an experiment to show how this is done, using nothing more than your eyes. Stand facing a building, which will take the place of the background of stars. Your eyes are the two observatories. Hold up your thumb at arm's length and sight on it against the building, closing first one eye and then the other (keep your arm quite still!). Notice how your thumb seems to "jump over" as you change from one eye to the other.

Just a few years ago, scientists found still another way to get the distance to the moon by seeing how long it takes for a radio signal to go there and bounce back. The distance found in this way proved to be the same as before.

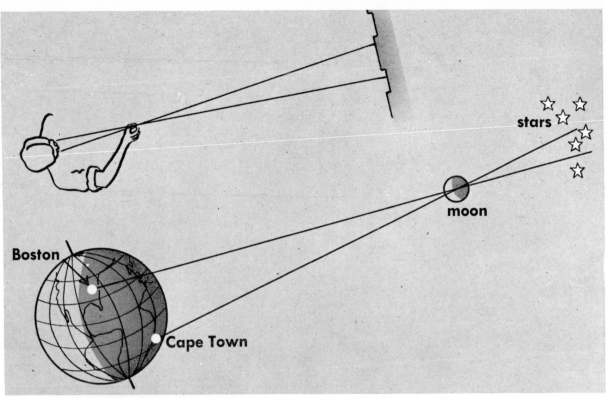

Finding the distance by sighting.

The thumb seems to "jump over."

THE MOON'S CHANGING FACE

If you look at the moon tonight and then again a few nights later, you will find that it looks a little different. The shape of the moon always seems to be changing and this is because of the way sunlight falls on it as it travels around the earth. These changes are called the *phases* of the moon, and the best way to understand why they happen is to do an experiment outdoors in the sunlight with the help of a rubber ball.

Suppose your head is the earth and the ball is the moon. Then, if you face toward the sun and hold the ball out in front of you, its dark side is toward you. This is what happens when the moon is at the place shown at the left side of the drawing, and the photograph beside it shows how the ball looks at that time. Astronomers call this phase "new moon."

About a week later the moon will be at the place shown at the bottom of the drawing. This is called "first quarter," because the moon has now gone a quarter of the way around its path. See this by holding the ball so that the sun is on your right and notice that only the right half of the ball catches sunlight.

By the time the moon is halfway around its path, the shape has gradually rounded out to a full, bright circle. This is "full moon." As the moon moves farther along, the light begins to fade off on the right side. When it gets to the place marked "last quarter," the sun is at the left and so only the left half of the moon is bright. Finally, after a whole month, it is new moon again and everything repeats.

Look in the newspaper to find out if the moon can be seen tonight and what phase it is in. Then, if possible, check this by looking at the moon itself.

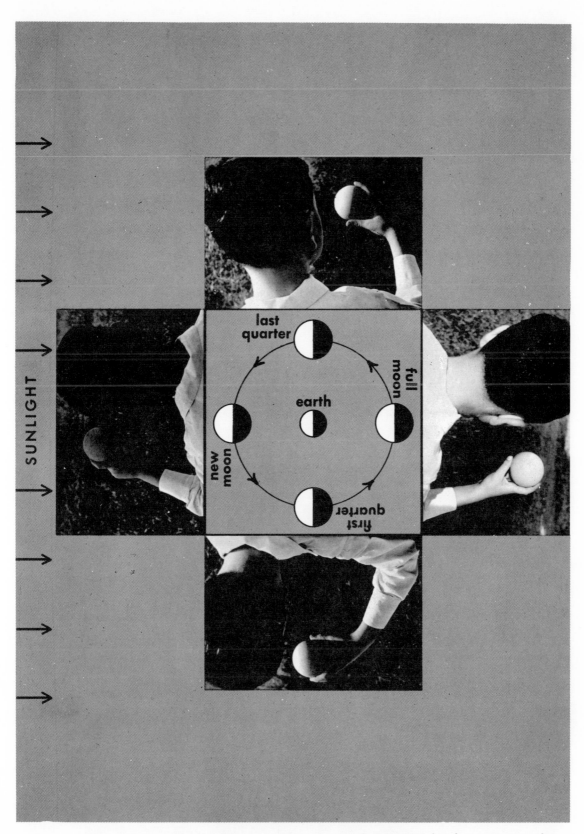

How the moon looks when seen from the earth. Turn the book to get one picture after another at the top.

THE MOON TURNS, TOO

Why does the moon always keep the same side toward the earth? This may sound as though the moon does not turn at all, but it is really always turning as it moves along its path around the earth.

Clear up this idea by pretending that you are the moon, and a post in your back yard is the earth. Move in a circle around the post, facing it all the while. The pictures show that in making a complete trip around the circle, you have faced in every direction, and yet the post has seen only the front of your body. So, although the moon makes a full turn on its own axis each time it goes around the earth, we have never seen the other side of the moon at all.

Astronomers believe that many millions of years ago the moon was spinning much faster than it does now. The pull of the earth gradually slowed down the spin until it finally got in step with the movement around the earth.

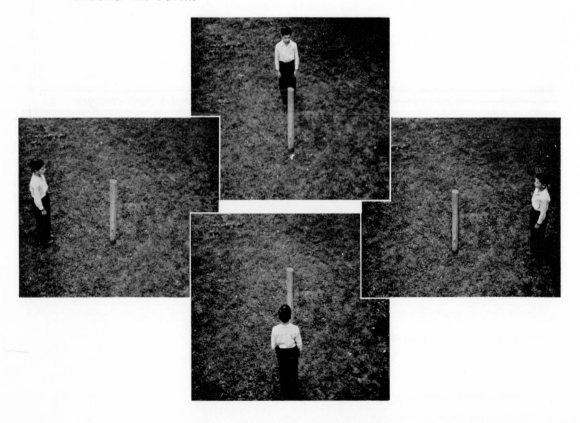

OUR SUN'S FAMILY

Look at the sky on a clear night and you will usually find at least one especially bright and steady star that does not seem to twinkle as much as the others. A few nights later you may be able to notice that this bright star has changed its position a little among the other stars near by. This is not a star at all, but one of the *planets*. A true star is a huge ball of white-hot gas like our sun, only much farther away, while a planet, like the earth, is a cooled-off ball of material. It does not send out light of its own but shines only because it reflects sunlight to us, just as the moon does.

Back in ancient times, people naturally thought that all the planets moved in circles around the earth. But the actual paths of the planets in the sky did not fit in with this idea and this puzzled everybody. Finally, when they began to realize that the sun, and not the earth, is the center around which all the planets move, everything could be explained perfectly. And now we know definitely that the earth and the other planets are members of the same family, all held by the pull of the sun.

Besides the big planets, there are about 1,500 much smaller planets, called *asteroids,* moving around the sun. They range in size from about one mile to a few hundred miles across, and a telescope is needed to see them. Astronomers believe they are either loose material left over when the big planets were formed, or else pieces of a big planet that broke up.

The solar system is the name given to the sun together with its family of planets, moons, comets and meteors all moving around it.

HERE ARE THE PLANETS

MERCURY

3,200 miles through the middle—less than half the size of the earth. 36,000,000 miles from the sun—closest planet to the sun. Mercury goes around the sun in 88 days. The sunny side is hotter than a furnace, while the other side is hundreds of degrees below zero. Certainly nothing could live there.

VENUS

7,800 miles across—a near twin to the earth in size. 67,000,000 miles from the sun—comes nearer to us than any other planet. Venus takes about 7½ months to go around the sun. Its temperature may be as high as boiling water, and very likely nothing could live there.

MARS

4,200 miles across. Nearly 142,000,000 miles from the sun. Mars takes 23 months to go around the sun. It has two tiny moons, one about 10 miles wide, the other only 5. This is the only planet that seems to have some air and water, and its queer markings, called "canals," may be plant life. Mars never gets warmer than one of our mild winter days but it gets as cold as "dry ice"—more than 120 degrees below zero.

JUPITER

89,000 miles across—the giant of the solar system. 484,000,000 miles from the sun—over 5 times as far as the earth. Jupiter takes nearly 12 years to complete a trip around the sun. It has 12 moons, 3 of them larger than our own. The temperature is about 200 degrees below zero and it is doubtful that anything could live there.

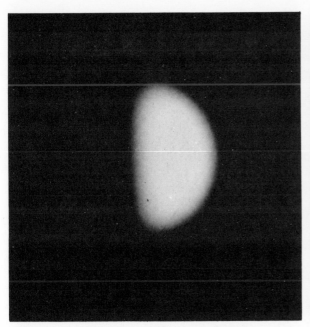

Mercury is the nearest planet to the sun.

Venus is probably covered with clouds all the time. Here it is seen as a crescent.

The white spot at Mars' pole is probably an icecap.

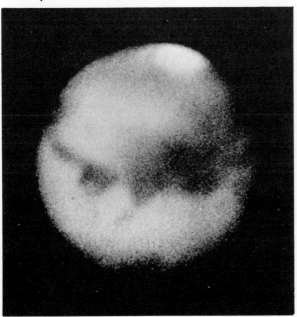

Jupiter's markings slowly change. They are probably clouds.

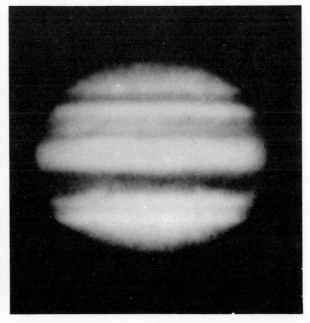

SATURN

75,000 miles across. 887,000,000 miles from the sun—nearly 10 times as far as the earth. Saturn's rings are made of countless small stones and are 170,000 miles across but only 10 miles thick. The planet goes around the sun in a little over 29 years. Besides being the only planet with rings, it has 9 moons. The temperature is about 250 degrees below zero and it is quite certain that nothing could live there.

URANUS

33,000 miles across. 1,780,000,000 miles from the sun—19 times the earth's distance. Uranus takes 84 years to circle the sun. It has 5 moons. It is safe to say that nothing could live on Uranus because its temperature is about 300 degrees below zero.

NEPTUNE

31,000 miles across. Almost 2,800,000,000 miles from the sun—30 times as far as the earth. Neptune takes nearly 165 years to go around the sun. It has 2 moons, one of them nearly three-quarters the size of our earth. The temperature is down around 350 degrees below zero, so certainly nothing could live there.

PLUTO

About 4,000 miles across. 3,680,000,000 miles from the sun—nearly 40 times the earth's distance. Pluto takes nearly 250 years to go around the sun. No moons have been discovered. The temperature is probably close to 400 degrees below zero because sunlight at this distance is almost 2,000 times weaker than on earth. Surely nothing could live there.

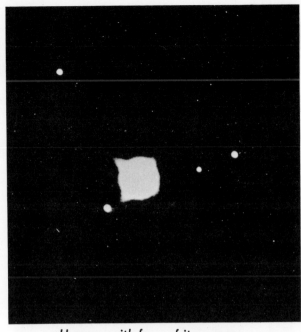

Saturn, like Jupiter, seems to be covered with streaky clouds.

Uranus, with four of its moons.

Neptune and its larger moon.

These two pictures, taken 24 hours apart, show how Pluto moves as seen against the stars.

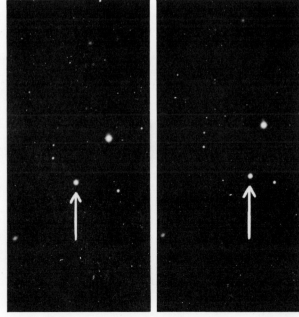

A LAYOUT OF THE SOLAR SYSTEM

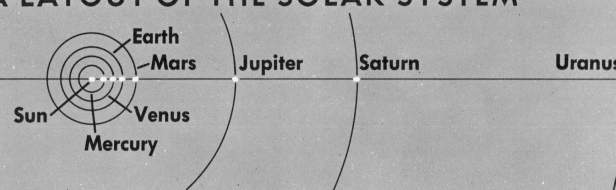

The planets move around the sun on paths that are slightly flattened circles. The drawing at the top of the page shows how these paths compare in size. Instead of whole circles for the farther planets, the drawing gives only a small section but this is all you need in order to get a good idea of the distances.

John wanted to make a really large chart that he could mount on the wall of his room, so he "scaled up" the one shown here. You can do the same thing as an interesting project. Use a piece of white shelf paper about 45 inches long. Rule a light pencil line straight along the center of the strip. Mark a dot on this line about 3 inches from the left edge of the paper, and this will be the sun.

You are going to scale up your drawing to make it exactly three times as big as the one above. To do this, mark the distance from the sun to each planet along the edge of a strip of paper placed on the chart at the top of this page. Then carefully mark off each distance *three times* on your drawing and make a dot.

Use a drawing compass to make the complete circles for Mercury, Venus, the Earth and Mars, and for the part circle of Jupiter's path. For

Neptune

Pluto

on this scale, the nearest star
is almost a mile and a half away ⟶

the farther planets, use a piece of string as a compass. Stick a pin firmly in the sun's dot. Ask someone to hold the point of a pencil on one of the planet dots while you tie the string in a tight loop around the pin and pencil. Now draw the section of the circle, as John is doing in the picture.

Go over the lines with a crayon. Letter the name of each planet, its distance from the sun and the time it takes to go around its path (see pages 24 and 26), and your chart is finished.

John uses a loop of string to draw the circles.

MODELING THE PLANETS

Mercury   **Venus**   **Earth**   **Mars**   **Jupiter**

Here is an astronomy project for making a set of models of the planets which will give you a good idea of their sizes. Each planet will be a ball of modeling clay and the sizes are chosen so that you can use a basketball as the sun. If you do not have one, you can use a beach ball or blow up a rubber balloon to the proper size. A basketball is about 10 inches through the middle.

To make a model of a planet, take a lump of clay that seems to be the right size and roll it lightly between the palms of your hands until it is evenly round, then hold it over the planet's outline at the top of this page to see if the size is right. If not, pinch off some clay, or add a bit, and roll again until the size matches the drawing. Stick pins into a board, as in the picture, to hold the finished clay balls.

Cut Saturn's ring out of cardboard. Set your compass points one inch apart for the outer edge of the ring and just a little more than half an inch apart to make the inner hole. Stick three small pieces of a toothpick into the clay, spacing them evenly around Saturn's equator, and put a tiny dab of glue on each to hold the ring in place.

Make a small label giving each planet's name and size, place the sun behind the whole set and you have your complete "midget model" of the solar family.

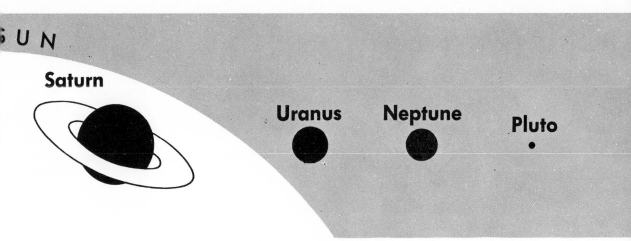

SUN

Saturn

Uranus **Neptune** **Pluto**

Notice how small the planets are, compared with the sun. If all the planets were rolled together, the sun would still be almost 600 times larger in bulk than this single lump of clay. And when you think of how far apart the planets really are, you begin to see how much empty space there is in the solar system.

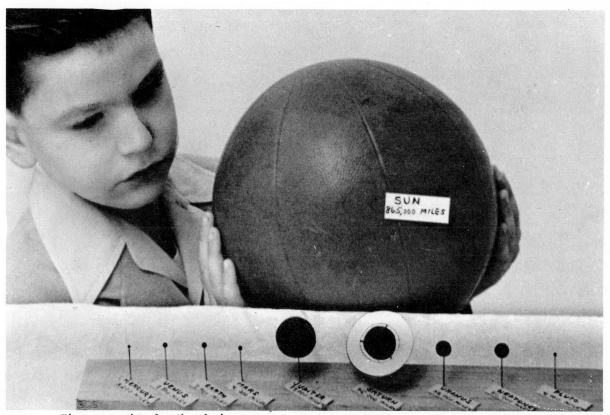

The sun and its family of planets.

WATCHING FOR THE PLANETS

The only planets that can be seen without a telescope are Mercury, Venus, Mars, Jupiter and Saturn. Even though you cannot see any of the markings and other details that show in a large telescope, you will find it interesting to locate some of the planets.

Remember, the best way to pick out the planets is by the steadiness of their light. Once you find a planet, look regularly every few nights to keep track of it. Notice that it moves slowly westward with the whole sky and also, as the weeks pass, it gradually changes its place as seen among the stars.

JUPITER shines with a true white light. Look for it in autumn in the southeastern sky and in winter in the southwest. A good field glass will show the four brightest of its moons, close to the planet.

SATURN is found in the southeastern sky in spring and in the southwest in summer. You will know it by its bright yellow-white color. Do not expect to see the rings; it takes a telescope to show them at all.

MARS shines with a reddish light. Being closer to the sun than Jupiter or Saturn, it changes its place in the sky much faster, so in order to locate it you will have to look up its position. The *World Almanac* in your library gives this information.

VENUS is brilliant white, far brighter at times than even the other planets. Like Mars, it changes its position greatly so you will have to locate it with the help of an almanac. Venus shows phases like our moon (page 21) but you need a telescope to see this.

MERCURY, being very close to the sun, is not easy to find. The best time to search for it is just after sunset in March or April. A field glass will help. Mercury, too, shows phases when seen in a telescope.

METEORS AND METEORITES

If you watch the sky on a clear, moonless night, the chances are very good that you will see a few *meteors*, sometimes called "shooting stars." These are not stars at all, but bits of stone that are usually no bigger than an apple seed. When one of them dives toward our earth with a hundred times the speed of a bullet, it rubs against the air so hard that it becomes white hot. Within a few seconds it burns up altogether, and this leaves the bright streak that you see. Over the entire earth several billion of these visitors come in every day.

At certain times of the year the earth runs into thick swarms of these stones and when this happens you sometimes can see several flashes a minute. This is called a "meteoric shower." Especially bright showers can usually be seen each year between about August 9th and 13th in the northeast, around October 19th to 23rd in the east and about December 10th to 13th in the east. Your newspaper may have some information on the meteoric showers around these times.

Once in a great while a much larger stone comes into our air and does not burn up completely before hitting the earth. Some of these scarred and pitted stones, called *meteorites*, can be seen in museums. Giant meteorites like the one in the picture are very rare.

This giant meteorite, weighing 36½ tons, can be seen in the American Museum of Natural History in New York City. It was brought down from Greenland by Commander Peary, discoverer of the North Pole.

COMETS

During your whole lifetime you may not see even a single comet in the sky, although half a dozen or so are sighted each year by astronomers with the help of telescopes. In ancient times, superstitious people thought that the coming of a comet was a warning that something dreadful was going to happen. Today we know that comets are made of ordinary materials, and that they have nothing at all to do with what happens on earth.

A comet usually has a fuzzy, glowing head and a long, wispy tail like the one in the picture. The head may be much larger in size than the whole earth, although it is not solid but is thought to be a loose swarm of stones mixed with dust and gas. A comet's tail is so thin that the stars shine right through it with hardly any weakening. At times, the tail may be several million miles long, while at other times it may almost disappear.

Comets truly belong to the solar system, for they move around the sun. Their paths are usually very long ovals, sometimes reaching out beyond Pluto. Several comets regularly come back to the neighborhood of the sun. Others, after appearing a few times, failed to return again, and some of these seem to have broken up into swarms of meteors, probably after coming too close to one of the large outer planets.

There is not much chance of a comet's hitting the earth. Even if this should happen, most of the solid pieces would burn up in the air and we would have nothing worse than a very thrilling shower of meteors.

Halley's Comet. It is expected to visit us again in 1986.

THE SUN

If someone should ask you what you consider the most important thing in the sky, you would have to say, "The sun." Without the light and heat that the sun gives us we would not be here at all. Every form of life on earth, both plant and animal, needs sunlight in order to exist.

Earlier in this book you found that the sun is a great ball of white-hot gas located about 93,000,000 miles away from the earth. It is so big that it would take more than a hundred earths side by side to stretch across its face.

By measuring its brightness, astronomers have been able to tell how hot the sun is. It turns out to be over 10,000 degrees, and this is the temperature of just the outer part. Deep inside the sun it must be many millions of degrees!

Most of the time we think of the sun only as a general glare in the sky, but when it is seen through a fog or at sunset, the roundness and sharpness of its appearance are surprising. **Never look at the sun direct** or you may permanently damage your eyes.

From time to time, jagged dark blotches, called *sun spots,* appear on the face of the sun. These are giant whirlpools in the outer gases, and the only reason they look dark is that they are cooler than the rest of the sun's face. An odd fact about sun spots is that they appear and disappear in a regular way. About every eleven years there are more of them than usual, and in between times they slack off. Weather conditions on earth seem to go along with these changes.

By using special instruments, astronomers are able to see great rose-colored clouds of gas spurting up around the edge of the sun (see picture). These clouds are named *prominences*. Sometimes they swirl up with speeds of several hundred miles a second and then seem to be sucked down again into the sun. The cause of these queer actions is not yet explained.

Around the edge of the sun is a silvery haze called the *corona*. Usually this can be seen only when the main ball of the sun is hidden by the moon during an eclipse (page 45). But astronomers do not have to wait for an eclipse. They can see the corona any time by using a special form of telescope. Many things remain to be found out about this mysterious outer part of the sun.

It is a mistake to think that the sun's heat is caused by something *burning up*. The sun does not burn like coal but only *glows* like an electric light. Air is needed to burn something and there is no air inside a lamp bulb or on the sun, so we must look for some other cause for the heat of the sun. Scientists now feel that they know what it is. The answer may surprise you: What happens deep inside the sun is really the same as the action of a hydrogen-bomb explosion. In this action, and in that of an atom bomb as well, some part of the material is changed directly into heat. This means that the atoms of the sun are being used up in order to keep sending out heat and light. The rate is figured out to be about 4,000,000 tons each second. But the sun is so huge that it could go on for billions of years at this rate before all its atoms would be gone.

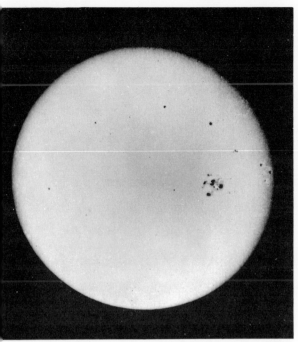

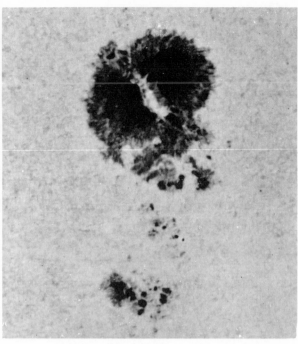

Sometimes many sunspots can be seen through the telescope.

You could drop the whole earth into this sunspot, with room to spare.

This enormous prominence reached up nearly 350,000 miles from the sun.

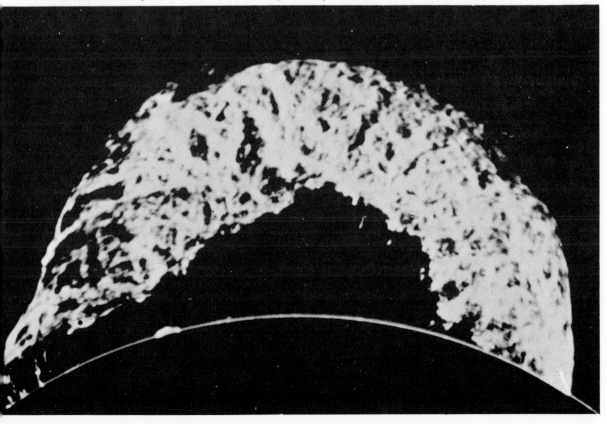

HOW TO MAKE A SUN CAMERA

You can make a kind of camera that will throw a light-picture on a piece of paper to show clearly the sharp round edge of the sun. The light-picture formed by any camera is called an *image*.

In order to find out how the sun camera works, start by making a small *pinhole camera*. It gets this name because it does not have a glass lens but uses instead a small hole to form an image.

Stretch a piece of wax paper across the open end of an oatmeal box, fastening it with a rubber band as in the picture. Punch a clean hole through the center of the other end of the box with a steel knitting needle. Now, if you hold this camera with the hole pointing toward any bright object, such as a lighted candle, you will see a true image of the flame on the wax-paper screen. Look carefully at the drawing and see if you can tell why the image is upside down, and why it gets bigger when you move the camera closer.

Now you are ready to set up a sun camera that uses the same idea. Make a clean hole in the center of a large sheet of stiff cardboard by pushing a pencil clear through it. Nail the cardboard to a stick and fasten it to a window sill upstairs, or to an upper porch, with the cardboard facing directly at the sun. Do this at a time when the shadow of the cardboard hits the ground and not the wall. Then, if you go downstairs and hold a white paper in this shadow, you can catch the sun's image on it. This is not just a spot of light shining through the hole. It is a real image of the sun's face, just like that of the candle.

While you have the sun camera set up, go right on to the next experiment.

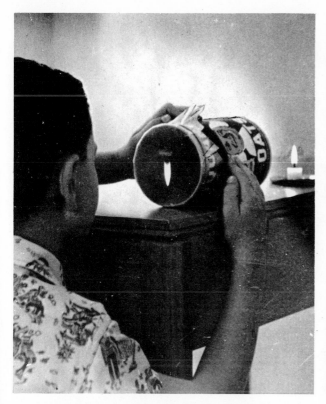

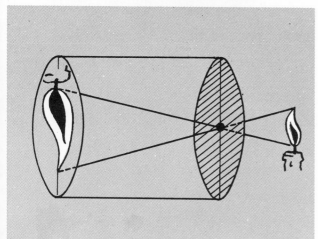

In the pinhole camera, you see the candle flame upside down. The drawing shows why.

The sun camera (see next page).

FINDING THE SIZE OF THE SUN

Use your sun camera to figure out the size of the sun itself. Here is what to do. Hold the white paper so it faces directly toward the hole in the cardboard and measure the width of the sun's image with a ruler. Then, using a long piece of string, find the distance between the white paper and the big cardboard upstairs. This distance will always turn out to be about 109 times the size of the sun's image.

When John tried the experiment, he found the image to be 2¾ inches across when the cardboard and the paper were 25 feet apart. Change 25 feet into inches by multiplying 25 by 12, and you have 300 inches. When you divide this by 2¾, which is the size of the image, the answer is just about 109. See if you can check this figure before you read on.

Now . . . how does this tell you the size of the sun? Astronomers have measured the distance from the earth to the sun by the same kind of "sighting" method described on page 18 for measuring the distance to the moon. They find that the sun is about 93,000,000 miles away from us. Just as the distance between the paper and the card is 109 times bigger than the sun's image, so is the distance from the earth to the sun 109 times the size of the sun itself, as the drawing shows. So, to get the actual distance across the sun, divide 93,000,000 by 109 and the answer is roughly 853,000, which is not far from the exact figure.

Don't worry if you have some trouble following the arithmetic all the way through. At least you will get the idea of how astronomers, by using clever methods, are able to measure things they cannot reach directly.

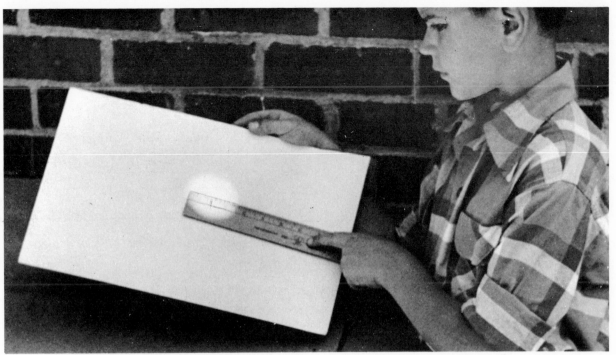

John measures the sun's image with a ruler.

How your sun camera works.

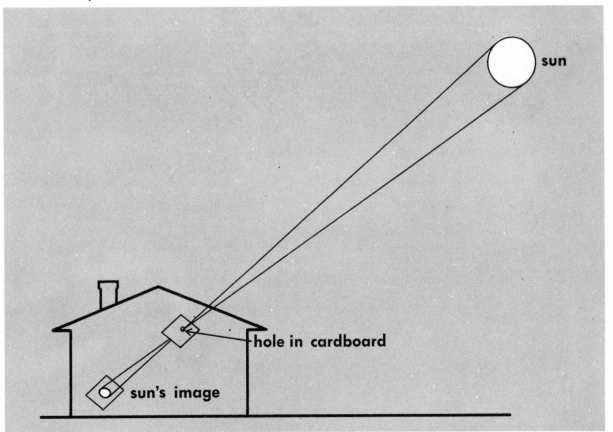

sun

hole in cardboard

sun's image

THE AIR BENDS SUNLIGHT

Everything we look at in the sky is seen by light that has had to travel through hundreds of miles of the air surrounding our earth. Before the light gets to us, many things can happen to it. The temperature of the air is never the same at all places and so the rays of light passing through it are bent aside in an uneven way. This causes the stars to twinkle, especially in winter when there are great differences in air temperatures.

Even when the air is very steady, it still makes us see things in a slightly different place in the sky from where they really are. Because of this, we are able to see the sun a couple of minutes before it comes up over the horizon at sunrise and after it has actually set.

You can set up an experiment to show how this happens. Fill a round jar to the very top with water, cover it tightly, and lay it on its side about a foot from the edge of a table. Stack up some books about two-thirds as high as the bottle and place them alongside it as in the picture. Take the bottle away and set a lighted candle on the table as shown. The candle should be short enough so that when you sight along the top of the books you cannot see the flame at all. Keeping your head in this position, put the bottle back alongside the books and you will now see the candle flame, even though it is below the level of the top of the books. Light from the flame had to curve to come to your eye.

The rounded top of the jar of water takes the place of the earth's air, and the candle is the sun. The sketch shows how the bending of rays of light brings the sun into view. This seeming "raising up" of the sun lets us see it for about five minutes longer each day than we would if air did not bend light.

The water in the bottle bends the light coming from the candle . . .

. . . just as the air bends light from the sun.

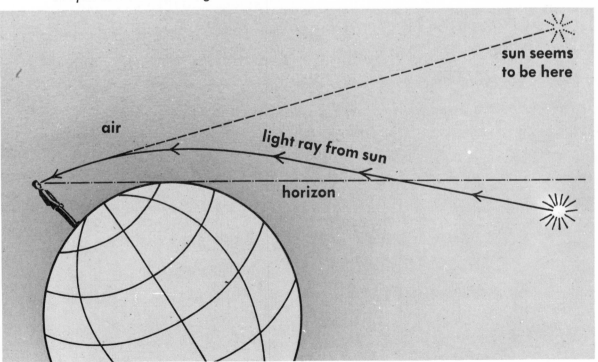

ECLIPSES

Everything that is lighted by the sun, including the earth and the moon, has a long pointed shadow trailing out behind it. You cannot tell that the shadow is there unless it falls on something, and then it shows up as a dark spot.

Sometimes the moon gets into the earth's shadow, as the drawing shows, and we call this an *eclipse* of the moon. It may stay in the shadow three or four hours. The moon, which is full at this time, still glows dull red because some sunlight is bent around into the shadow by our air (look back at page 43).

Because it travels on a slanting path, the moon does not go into the earth's shadow on every monthly trip. Most of the time it passes either above or below the shadow, missing it altogether, and so we have only one or two eclipses of the moon a year.

Much more thrilling than an eclipse of the moon is a total eclipse of the sun. As the drawing shows, this happens when the moon's shadow falls on the earth. The darkened spot is usually between fifty and a hundred miles wide. This shadow spot does not stay in one place but sweeps across the earth on a long curving path because the earth turns and the moon moves onward. If you happen to be in the path of the shadow, the sky will get dark, the sun will be hidden by the moon, and you will be able to see the beautiful corona. The sun may remain hidden for as much as several minutes.

Usually there are only one or two total eclipses of the sun each year and astronomers are able to figure out their times and paths hundreds of years ahead. An almanac or the newspaper will tell when and where the next eclipses of the moon or of the sun will happen.

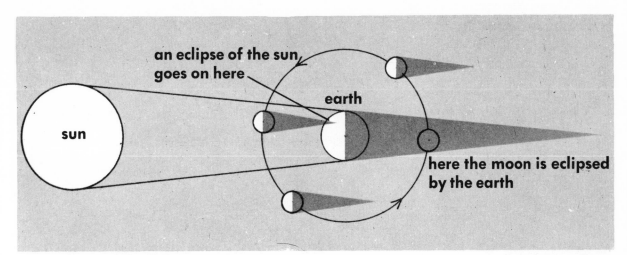

How eclipses happen.

The sun's corona can be seen at the time of a total eclipse, when the moon comes squarely between us and the sun.

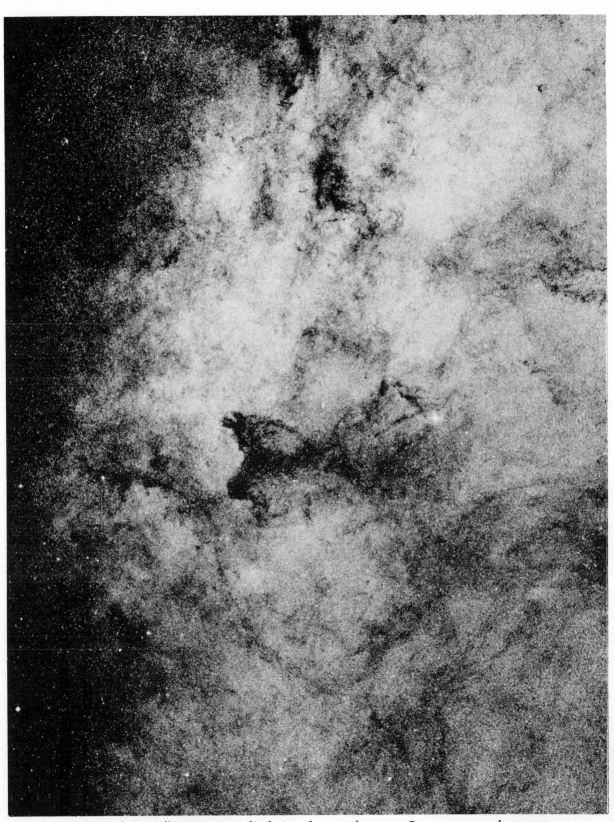

A part of the Milky Way, as it looks in a large telescope. Can you guess how many stars there are in the picture?

THE STARS

On a clear night there seem to be millions of stars in the sky, but actually you are able to see only two or three thousand separate ones. An opera glass or field glass will show up many more, and with large telescopes astronomers can see many millions of fainter stars.

Long ago, people who watched the sky imagined the stars to be grouped into outlines of familiar figures. They believed they saw such things as a warrior, an animal, or a crown, and so on. Such a group of stars is called a *constellation*.

Like our sun, the stars are huge globes of glowing gas, but so far away that they seem to be only tiny points of light. Some are hotter and brighter than the sun, and some are much cooler and dimmer. The smallest ones are not much bigger than the planets. The largest that have been measured are nearly 400 million miles across (see drawing on page 49).

The brightness of a star, as we see it, depends not only on how strongly it glows but also on how far away it is. Even the *nearest* star to the solar system is 25,000,000,000,000 (twenty-five trillion) miles away.

To make it easier to talk about such huge distances, astronomers use another measure called a *light year*. This is the distance that light would travel in one year's time, going at its usual rate of about eleven million miles a minute. A light year amounts to nearly 6,000,000,000,000 miles, so it is simpler to say that the nearest star is a little more than four light years from here. And how far away is the *farthest* star? Using the biggest telescopes, astronomers can find groups of stars that are billions of light years from us.

There is one star that seems to remain in place while all the others turn around it. This is because it happens to be almost directly above the North Pole of the earth, and it is called the Pole Star. To find it, we use the Big Dipper as a guide. Look up at the northern sky and you will easily find a group of bright stars arranged in the shape of a long-handled ladle. In summer, which is the best time to see the Dipper, its handle is turned upward so that the bowl would not "hold water." Now imagine a straight line running through the two stars in the end of the bowl, as in the drawing. Follow this line across about five times as far as the space between the two stars, and you will come to the Pole Star. Navigators of ships and planes use this star to get their bearings.

The Pole Star can be seen only by people living north of the equator. The constellations near the Pole Star remain in sight through the whole night as they circle around it. But others are seen rising in the east, moving across the sky as the night passes, and finally setting in the west.

Because the earth turns on its axis and at the same time travels around the sun, different constellations come into view at different times of the year. That is why there are certain times when it is best to look for each constellation.

In the next few pages you will meet a few interesting stars and constellations and learn how to find them in the sky. You will also get some idea of how the stars are spread out through space.

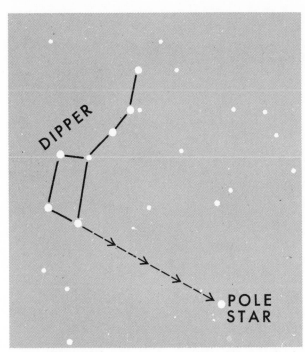

The Dipper's two "pointers" show how to find the Pole Star.

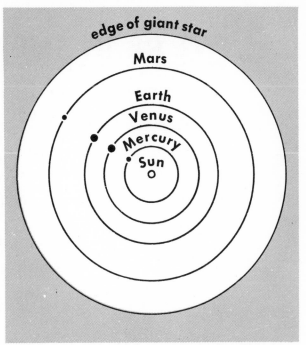

Some stars are so big that all the planets out as far as Mars could travel around inside them.

Long ago, people thought this constellation looked like a bear in the sky.

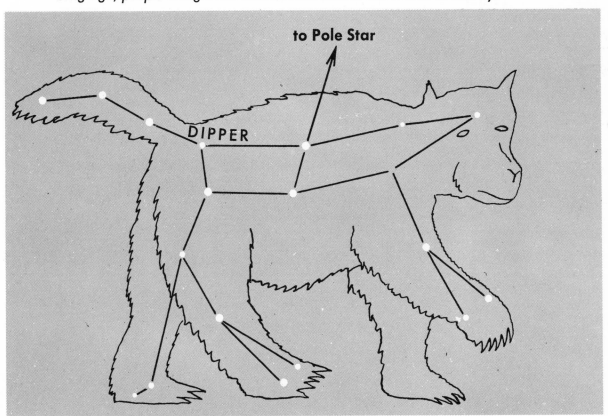

WE'RE IN THE MILKY WAY

On a clear night we can see a fuzzy, uneven band of light stretching across the sky. This hazy glow is called the Milky Way, and it is really made up of an enormous number of separate stars forming a huge flattened cloud that is shaped something like a fried egg. The sun and its planets are near the outer border at the place shown in the drawing. Because we are inside this "fried egg," we see many more stars when looking along the flat part of it than when looking in the up and down direction.

The whole group of stars forming the Milky Way is called the *Galaxy*. It is so big that it takes light about 100,000 years to cross from one edge to the other. It is made up of many billions of stars, of which one unimportant little one is our sun!

The picture on the opposite page, taken through a large telescope, shows the Andromeda Nebula. This is a galaxy outside our own, but much like it in shape. Notice how the dark streaks of dust and gas between the stars make it look like a huge whirlpool. This is probably what our own galaxy would look like if we could see it from the outside. Many of the stars in this shining swarm may have planets circling around them. And on some of these planets there may even be living creatures who wonder about the stars just as we do.

THE SUN

How our galaxy would look from the outside. All around the main part there are many clusters of stars.

The Andromeda Nebula is a galaxy very much like the one we are in.

SOME SIGHTS IN THE SKY

Many interesting things in the sky can be seen and studied with nothing more than your eyes. It is very helpful, of course, to have an ordinary opera glass or field glass. Do your looking on any clear night when the moon is away, and at a place where there is no glare from street lights. Use a flashlight to follow the star maps and drawings in the book, but cover the end of the lamp with a piece of colored cellophane or tissue paper to cut down the brightness.

First, look at the star at the bend of the handle of the Dipper. Right near it is a fainter star which you will easily discover. A telescope would show that the brighter star itself is a double, and by studying the light from this pair, astronomers find that one of them, in turn, is a double! Altogether, then, what seem to be only two stars at the bend of the Dipper's handle are really four.

Next, look for the star called Arcturus. You can find it whenever the handle of the Dipper is high in the sky. Summer is the best time. Follow the way the handle points, as the drawing shows, and you come to this bright star. Arcturus is cooler than the sun, and that is why it looks orange in color, while the sun looks white-hot. Arcturus is 38 light years from the earth. This means that the light by which you see it tonight left the star at about the time your parents were born.

The finest sight in the winter sky is the constellation Orion. Find it by looking for the three stars in a row that make up the "belt" of Orion. The chart shows how the bright reddish star Betelgeuse and the bright

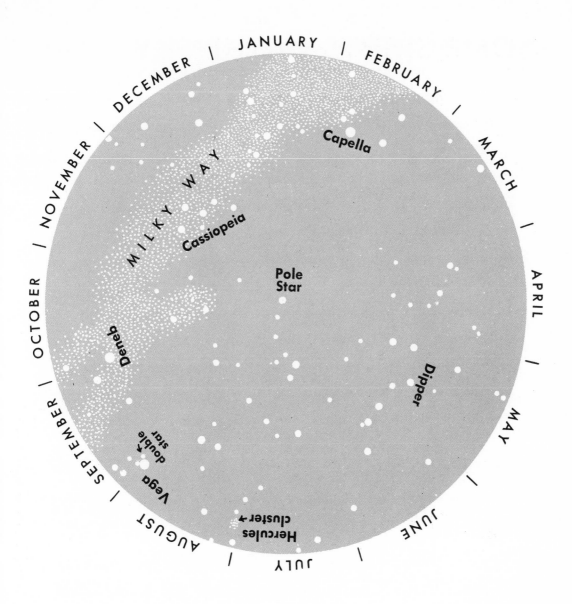

THE SKY AROUND THE POLE STAR

This chart shows most of the stars around the Pole Star that you can see with your eyes alone. The bigger the white dot, the brighter the star. To use the map, turn the book so that the present month is at the top, and hold the chart up toward the Pole Star in the sky. The map will then show how the stars look at about nine o'clock tonight.

blue-white star Rigel form a cross with the belt. Just below the belt there are three faint stars. The middle one, which looks fuzzy, is really a huge glowing mass of gas called the Orion Nebula, pictured on the opposite page. Just to the east of Orion is the bluish star Sirius, the brightest in the whole sky.

In late summer, look high in the northeast and you will see a group of stars shaped like a stretched-out letter "W." This constellation is called Cassiopeia. Off to the right (see the chart) you will just be able to see a fuzzy patch of faint light. Once you know where to look, an opera glass will help, but the true appearance of this patch is seen in the picture on page 51. It is the Andromeda Nebula.

Also in late summer, almost directly overhead, you will see a bright blue star named Vega. With two faint stars near by, it forms a triangle as shown on the star map on page 53. Look carefully at the star toward the east and you may be able to see that it is really double. A telescope shows that each of these is also a pair of stars, so here is a case of a "double double."

High in the eastern sky in autumn you can see a beautiful, sparkling little group of stars known as the Pleiades, sometimes called the Seven Sisters. The cluster is shaped like a little dipper. Only the brightest stars can usually be seen with the eye alone, but there are actually about 500 in the group. The main stars are shown in the chart opposite, together with the bright red star Aldebaran, which is not far away.

In August, directly overhead, you can see a faint patch of light called the Hercules cluster. The star map on page 53 will help you find it. An opera glass gives you a little better view but without a big telescope it is hard to realize that this is a swarm of about 100,000 stars, most of them much brighter than our sun.

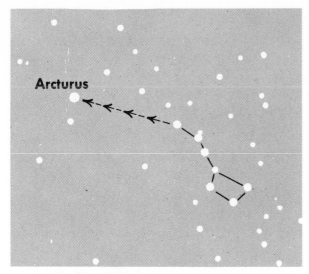

Finding Arcturus.

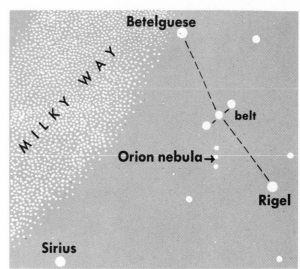

The constellation Orion.

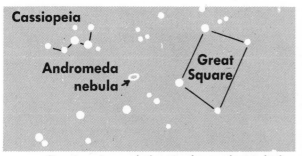

Cassiopeia and the Andromeda Nebula.

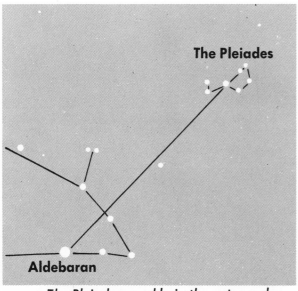

The Pleiades sparkle in the autumn sky.

The Orion Nebula.

THE UNIVERSE IS SWELLING UP

As large as it seems to us, the Galaxy is made up only of our *nearest* neighbor stars. Billions of other galaxies can be found with the biggest telescopes, and some are so far away that it takes their light nearly a billion years to get here. These huge galaxies, which seem to be scattered quite evenly through space, make up our *universe*—a word that means "everything that there is."

By studying the light from the distant galaxies it is possible to tell how far away they are and also how they are moving. Astronomers were greatly surprised to find that the galaxies all seem to be moving away from us at high speed, and the farthest ones are moving fastest. Einstein's Theory of Relativity explains this by saying that all of space itself is swelling up, carrying the galaxies along with it. There is nothing special about us here on earth that makes all the galaxies back away from us. We would see the same thing if we happened to be living in any of the other star groups. They are getting farther apart from each other all the time.

To see how this can be, do an interesting experiment. Make some marks on a toy balloon with a crayon or ink. The balloon itself stands for the universe and each spot is a galaxy in it. If you now blow the balloon up bigger, as John is doing in the picture, you notice that each spot moves away from all the others.

So this is what our universe is like, as far as scientists can tell. Most of us will not be satisfied with what we now know but will want to go on thinking and wondering about the universe, even though we realize that it is so big and so marvelous that our minds can never grasp it all.

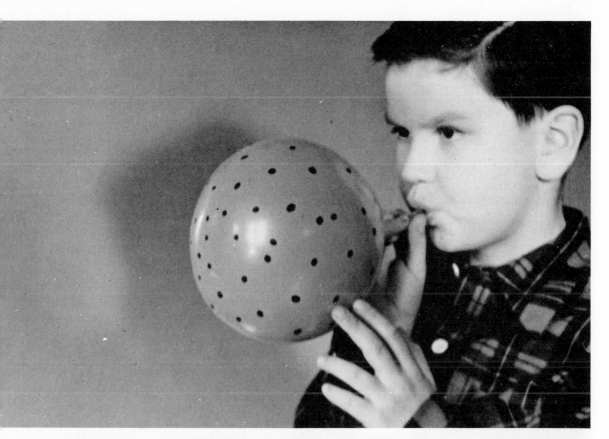

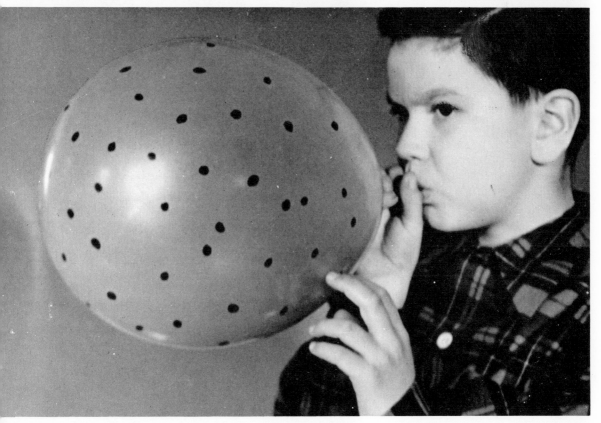

HOW TO PRONOUNCE
SOME OF THE WORDS IN THIS BOOK

Aldebaran	Al-DEB-ah-ran	Jupiter	JOO-pih-tur
Andromeda	Ann-DROM-eh-duh	Meteor	MEE-tee-uhr
Arcturus	Ark-TOO-russ	Nebula	NEB-yoo-luh
Asteroid	AS-tur-oyd	Orion	Oh-RY-unn
Betelgeuse	BEET-'l-juhz	Pleiades	PLEE-uh-deez
Cassiopeia	Kass-ee-oh-PEE-ah	Pluto	PLOO-toh
Comet	KOM-et	Rigel	RY-jel
Constellation	Kon-steh-LAY-shun	Saturn	SAT-urn
Corona	Ko-ROH-nuh	Sirius	SEER-ee-uss
Eclipse	Ee-KLIPS	Solar System	SO-l'r SIS-tem
Equator	Ee-KWAY-ter	Universe	YOO-nih-vurss
Galaxy	GAL-ak-see	Uranus	YOO-ra-nuss
Hercules	HURR-kyoo-leez	Vega	VEE-gah
Horizon	Ho-RY-zen	Venus	VEE-nuss